Pebble® Plus

Bilingüe/Bilingual

Investiga las estaciones/Investigate the Seasons

Veamos el invierno/ Let's Look at Winter

por/by Sarah L. Schuette

Traducción/Translation: Dr. Martín Luis Guzmán Ferrer
Editor Consultor/Consulting Editor: Dra. Gail Saunders-Smith

Capstone press®

Mankato, Minnesota

Pebble Plus is published by Capstone Press,
151 Good Counsel Drive, P.O. Box 669, Mankato, Minnesota 56002.
www.capstonepress.com

1 2 3 4 5 6 13 12 11 10 09 08

Library of Congress Cataloging-in-Publication Data
Schuette, Sarah L., 1976–
    [Let's look at winter. Spanish & English]
    Veamos el invierno / por Sarah L. Schuette = Let's look at winter / by Sarah L. Schuette.
    p. cm. — (Pebble Plus. Investiga las estaciones = Investigate the seasons)
    Includes index.
    ISBN-13: 978-1-4296-2291-2 (hardcover)
    ISBN-10: 1-4296-2291-1 (hardcover)
    1. Animal behavior — Juvenile literature. 2. Winter — Juvenile literature. I. Title. II. Title: Let's look at
winter. III. Series.
QL753.S38418 2009
508.2 — dc22   2008004829

Summary: Simple text and photographs present what happens to the weather, animals, and plants in winter —
    in both English and Spanish.

Editorial Credits
Martha E. H. Rustad, editor; Katy Kudela, bilingual editor; Adalín Torres-Zayas, Spanish copy editor;
    Bobbi J. Wyss, set designer; Veronica Bianchini, book designer; Kara Birr, photo researcher;
    Scott Thoms, photo editor

Photo Credits
Corbis/Donna Disario, cover (background tree)
Getty Images Inc./The Image Bank/Joseph Van Os, 12–13; The Image Bank/LWA, 5
iStockphoto Inc./Jonathan Clark, 19
Peter Arnold/Angelika Jakob, 20–21
Shutterstock/bora ucak, cover, 1 (magnifying glass); Doxa, 9; Ilya D. Gridnev, cover (inset leaf); Jeff Thrower
    (WebThrower), 16–17; Tim Elliott, 11; Tony Campbell, 15
SuperStock/age fotostock, 1 (snowballs); Tom Benoit, 7

The author dedicates this book to her friend Elizabeth Haugen Todd of Hutchinson, Minnesota.

Note to Parents and Teachers

The Investiga las estaciones/Investigate the Seasons set supports national science
standards related to weather and climate. This book describes and illustrates winter in
both English and Spanish. The images support early readers in understanding the text.
The repetition of words and phrases helps early readers learn new words. This book also
introduces early readers to subject-specific vocabulary words, which are defined in the
Glossary section. Early readers may need assistance to read some words and to use the
Table of Contents, Glossary, Internet Sites, and Index sections of the book.

Table of Contents

It's Winter! 4

Animals in Winter 10

Plants in Winter. 16

What's Next? 20

Glossary 22

Internet Sites 24

Index 24

Tabla de contenidos

¡Es invierno!. 4

Los animales en invierno 10

Las plantas en invierno 16

¿Qué le sigue?. 20

Glosario. 23

Sitios de Internet. 24

Índice 24

It's Winter!

How do you know it's winter? The temperature is cold.

¡Es invierno!

¿Cómo sabemos que es invierno? El clima es frío.

The ground hardens.

Water freezes.

When snow falls,

it covers everything.

La tierra se pone dura.

El agua se congela.

Cuando la nieve cae,

lo cubre todo.

The sun rises later in the morning. Winter days are the shortest of the year.

El Sol sale más tarde por la mañana. Los días de invierno son los más cortos del año.

cortos del año.

invierno son los más

la mañana. Los días de

El Sol sale más tarde por

the shortest of the year.

morning. Winter days are

The sun rises later in the

9

Animals in Winter

What do animals do
in winter? Deer search
for food under the snow.

Los animales en invierno

¿Qué es lo que hacen
los animales en invierno?
Los venados buscan comida
debajo de la nieve.

Brown rabbits turn white.
Now their fur blends in
with the snow.

Los conejos de color marrón
se ponen blancos. Así su
pelo es como la nieve.

Cardinals sit in evergreen
trees. They stay for the whole
winter. Some birds migrate.

Los cardenales se sientan
en los árboles perennes.
Se quedan todo el invierno.
Algunos pájaros migran.

Plants in Winter

What happens to plants in winter? They do not grow. Many plants look bare and brown.

Las plantas en invierno

¿Qué les pasa a las plantas en invierno? No crecen. Muchas plantas se ven desnudas y secas.

Evergreen trees stay green.
They keep their needles
all year round.

Los árboles perennes siempre
están verdes. Los pinos tienen
sus agujas todo el año.

19

What's Next?

The temperature gets warmer. Winter is over. What season is next?

¿Qué le sigue?

El clima se empieza a poner más templado. Ha terminado el invierno. ¿Cuál es la siguiente estación?

Glossary

bare — not covered

evergreen — a tree or bush that has green needles all year long

freeze — to become solid or icy at a very low temperature

migrate — to move from one place to another when seasons change

needle — a sharp, green leaf on an evergreen tree

season — one of the four parts of the year; winter, spring, summer, and fall are seasons.

temperature — the measure of how hot or cold something is

Glosario

la aguja — la hoja verde y puntiaguda de un árbol perenne

el clima — las condiciones a la intemperie en cierta época del año o lugar; el clima cambia con cada estación.

congelado — cuando algo se pone sólido o helado a temperaturas muy bajas

desnuda — que no ésta cubierta

la estación — una de las cuatro épocas del año; el invierno, la primavera, el verano y el otoño son estaciones.

migrar — moverse de un lado a otro cuando cambian las estaciones

perenne — árbol o arbusto que tiene verdes las agujas todo el año

Internet Sites

FactHound offers a safe, fun way to find Internet sites related to this book. All of the sites on FactHound have been researched by our staff.

Here's how:

1. Visit *www.facthound.com*

2. Choose your grade level.

3. Type in this book ID **1429622911** for age-appropriate sites. You may also browse subjects by clicking on letters, or by clicking on pictures and words.

4. Click on the **Fetch It** button.

FactHound will fetch the best sites for you!

Index

animals, 10, 12, 14

bare, 16

cardinals, 14

cold, 4

days, 8

deer, 10

evergreen trees, 14, 18

food, 10

freezing, 6

fur, 12

growing, 16

migrating, 14

needles, 18

plants, 14, 16, 18

rabbits, 12

snow, 6, 10, 12

sun, 8

temperature, 4, 20

warm, 20

Sitios de Internet

FactHound te brinda una manera divertida y segura de encontrar sitios de Internet relacionados con este libro. Hemos investigado todos los sitios de FactHound. Es posible que algunos sitios no estén en español.

Se hace así:

1. Visita *www.facthound.com*

2. Elige tu grado escolar.

3. Introduce este código especial **1429622911** para ver sitios apropiados a tu edad, o usa una palabra relacionada con este libro para hacer una búsqueda general.

4. Haz un clic en el botón **Fetch It**.

¡FactHound buscará los mejores sitios para ti!

Índice

agujas, 18

animales, 10, 12, 14

árboles perennes, 14, 18

cardenales, 14

clima, 4, 20

comida, 10

conejos, 12

congelado, 6

crecer, 16

desnudas, 16

días, 8

frío, 4

migrar, 14

nieve, 6, 10, 12

pelo, 12

plantas, 14, 16, 18

Sol, 8

templado, 20

venados, 10